START-UP
ENGLISH
BIOGRAPHIES

DICK
KING-SMITH

Chris Powling

Evans

Evans Brothers Limited

Published by Evans Brothers Limited
2A Portman Mansions
Chiltern Street
London W1U 6NR

Acknowledgements: All photographs by Richard Newton except page 21 Corbis/Everett

Printed in China

Editor: Bryony Jones
Designer: Mark Holt

British Library Cataloguing in Publication Data

Powling, Chris.
    Dick King-Smith. – (Start-up English. Biographies)
    1. King-Smith, Dick – Juvenile literature. 2. Novelists,
    English--20th century – Biography--Juvenile literature.
    I. Title II. Series
    823.9'14-dc22

ISBN-13: 9780237539023

Contents

Who is Dick King-Smith?

Dick King-Smith is a **famous author**. Children all over the world love his books about bossy parrots, hens that attack foxes, and hedgehogs who don't know how to cross the road....

He started writing quite late in life. Here's the story of his life so far.

famous   author

▲ Dick lives in Somerset, in a house that is more than 350 years old. It is only a few miles from where he was born.

School and childhood

Dick had a happy **childhood**. 'There wasn't much traffic,' he says, 'so I was able to **roam** the countryside on my bike.'

He also loved reading, especially animal stories.

◀ Dick, aged four, with his grandfather, aged 102, and his grandmother and mother

childhood   roam

Dick went to the famous **public school**, Marlborough, and studied **Latin** and **Greek**. 'But what I really wanted to do was live on a farm.'

So did **Myrle**, the girl he wanted to marry.

▶ **Dick's favourite dog, Susie**

War breaks out

Then World War Two started, so Dick and Myrle could not marry yet. And farming had to wait too.

▲ Dick and Myrle in their war-time uniforms.

Myrle joined the **RAF** to help spot **enemy** planes.

Dick joined the army. He went to Italy, where he was badly **wounded** and sent home.

After the war

▶ **Dick and Myrle married during the war in 1943.**

After the war they were lucky. Dick says, 'My father's **firm** bought a farm. They asked me to **manage** it.'

firm   **manage**

The milk, eggs and bacon from the farm were eaten at the firm's canteen.

▲ Dick and Myrle had three children. This picture shows them as adults. They are called Juliet, Giles and Lizzie.

canteen

Farming... and disaster!

On the farm, Dick milked the cows and looked after the pigs and hens. Foxes often attacked his hens. Poor hens! How could they fight back? This gave him an idea for a story.

idea

But before he could write his story down, **disaster** struck. Dick's farm had to close.

▲ He tried different jobs, until he became a **teacher** at this primary school.

disaster   teacher

Writing stories

Dick liked teaching children a lot, and he liked the reading and writing. But he didn't like the number work. Perhaps this is why he went back to his story, which he wrote during the summer holidays.

DICK KING-SMITH

The Fox Busters

Puffin|Modern|Classics

◀ It was called 'The Fox Busters'.

▲ Dick felt very grateful to his wife, Myrle,
who encouraged him to write the story.

Dick's next book was 'Daggie Dogfoot', about
his favourite animals, pigs.

grateful   encouraged

Being a famous author!

Before long, Dick had written lots more stories. 'The Sheep-Pig' won a big prize.

▲ He soon won many more awards.

◀ Dick and Myrle are dressed up to celebrate!

prize   awards   celebrate

About this time Dick appeared regularly on the children's TV series 'Rub-A-Dub-Tub' and 'Pob'.

▲ He was very famous after this. So was his pet dog, Dodo.

regularly

How does he write his stories?

Soon Dick was writing about eight stories a year. He has written more than 100 books, and sold more than five million copies worldwide.

▶ Each morning, Dick climbed up to his writing room.

copies   worldwide

Dick's writing room was full of books and pictures.

▶ He used to write on rough paper for about two hours.

◀ In the afternoon, he typed out what he had written on a very old typewriter!

typewriter   19

New ideas

Dick was always thinking of new ideas for stories, even when he was resting in his armchair or enjoying his garden. 'Lots of ideas come whizzing into my mind. Most are so batty I chuck them out again.'

▶ Dick with some artwork from his books

mind   artwork

Watch out for Dick's stories on television and as films at your local cinema.

◀ Farmer Hogget and Babe... in the film based on Dick's book 'The Sheep-Pig'.

Dick has now retired from writing books, although you never know when a new idea will pop up!

local   retired

Further information for

Key words introduced in the text

artwork	disaster	idea	RAF	worldwide
author	encouraged	Latin	regularly	World War Two
awards	enemy	local	retired	wounded
canteen	famous	manage	roam	
celebrate	firm	miles	teacher	
childhood	grateful	prize	typewriter	
copies	Greek	public school	uniforms	

Background Information

Pages 6 and 7

Dick's father ran a family business making paper, which owned the farm that Dick later ran. Dick had a brother, who was called Tony.

Dick loved reading, and as well as reading animal stories he read the 'William' stories by Richmal Crompton. About school, he says, 'I was reasonably intelligent… and reasonably lazy.' But he really wanted to live on a farm.

Pages 8 and 9

Dick and Myrle first met when they were only 13. Their families were close friends. Dick says, 'I was annoyed with her at first because she could throw stones further than I could. She was better at breeding budgies, too. This was one of our hobbies.'

During the war, Dick was sent to Italy as a Guards Officer.

There, he fought at the Salerno landings. Just south of Florence he was badly wounded, and so eventually he had to be sent home.

Pages 10 and 11

While Dick and Myrle's family was growing, and they were working on the farm, Dick began to write poems for fun. Some of them were printed in magazines like 'Punch', 'The Field' and 'Good Housekeeping'.

Dick's children are now grown-ups, and he also has 11 grandchildren and one great-grandchild.

Pages 12 and 13

After Dick's farm closed, he tried working at another farm as a tenant farmer, but this closed too. 'I wasn't any good at the money-making side of farming,' he says.

Before becoming a teacher, Dick tried selling fire-fighting suits and working in a shoe factory.

Parents and Teachers

Topics for discussion

Discuss your favourite Dick King-Smith books, giving reasons. Why do you think Dick's books have become so famous?

Sometimes things happen that we do not enjoy, for example when Dick's farm had to close. But this can lead to new opportunities, like encouraging Dick to start writing books. Can you think of any times when something bad turned into something good?

Suggested activities

Ask the children to write and illustrate a review of one of Dick King-Smith's books.
Listen to Dick King-Smith talk about his books at
http://www.4learning.co.uk/sites/bookbox/authors/kingsmith/clips.htm

Recommended resources

All About Dick King-Smith, Vic Parker, Heinemann Library, 2005
http://www.4learning.co.uk/sites/bookbox/writerstoolkit/home.htm
http://www.4learning.co.uk/sites/bookbox/authors/kingsmith/index.htm
http://www.randomhouse.com/kids/dickkingsmith/interview.html
http://www.randomhouse.com/teachers/catalog/display.pperl?isbn=9780375814594&view=tg
http://www.bbc.co.uk/bigtoe/authors/kingsmith/

Important dates

1922	Dick King-Smith is born
1936-40	Goes to Marlborough College, Wiltshire
1941-46	War service in the Grenadier Guards
1943	Marries Myrle
1947-61	Runs farm for his father's company
1961	Father's company closes down
1961-67	Tenant farmer
1967-71	Dick works as a salesman, then in a shoe factory
1971-75	Trains to be a teacher at Bristol University
1975-82	Class teacher at Farmborough Primary School, Bath
1978	He publishes 'The Fox Busters'
1982	Becomes a full-time writer
1984	'The Sheep-Pig' wins the Guardian Award
1983-88	Dick appears regularly on television in 'Rub-A-Dub-Tub' and 'Pob'
1992	Voted Children's Author of the Year
1995	He wins the Children's Book Award
1996	The film 'Babe' is made from 'The Sheep-Pig'
2000	Myrle, Dick's wife, dies
2001	Publishes his autobiography, 'Chewing the Cud'

Index